DUDLEY SCHOOLS
LIBRARY SERVICE

KU-709-620

Schools Library and Information Services

S00000705922

We Are All Different

We All Communicate

Rebecca Rissman

Heinemann
LIBRARY

www.heinemannlibrary.co.uk
Visit our website to find out more information about Heinemann Library books.

To order:
 Phone 44 (0) 1865 888066
 Send a fax to 44 (0) 1865 314091
 Visit the Heinemann Bookshop at www.heinemannlibrary.co.uk to browse our catalogue and order online.

Heinemann Library is an imprint of Capstone Global Library Limited, a company incorporated in England and Wales having its registered office at 7 Pilgrim Street, London, EC4V 6LB – Registered company number: 6695582

Heinemann is a registered trademark of Pearson Education Limited, under licence to Capstone Global Library Limited

Text © Capstone Global Library Limited 2009
First published in hardback in 2009
The moral rights of the proprietor have been asserted.

All rights reserved. No part of this publication may be reproduced in any form or by any means (including photocopying or storing it in any medium by electronic means and whether or not transiently or incidentally to some other use of this publication) without the written permission of the copyright owner, except in accordance with the provisions of the Copyright, Designs and Patents Act 1988 or under the terms of a licence issued by the Copyright Licensing Agency, Saffron House, 6–10 Kirby Street, London EC1N 8TS (www.cla.co.uk). Applications for the copyright owner's written permission should be addressed to the publisher.

Edited by Rebecca Rissman, Charlotte Guillain and Catherine Veitch
Designed by Joanna Hinton-Malivoire
Picture research by Tracy Cummins
Production by Duncan Gilbert
Originated by Dot Gradations Ltd
Printed and bound in China by South China Printing Company Ltd

ISBN 978 0 431 19310 6 (hardback)
13 12 11 10 09
10 9 8 7 6 5 4 3 2 1

PUBLIC LIBRARIES
705922   SCH
J001.5

British Library Cataloguing in Publication Data
Rissman, Rebecca
We all communicate. - (We are all different)
1. People with disabilities - Means of communication - Juvenile literature
305.9'08
A full catalogue record for this book is available from the British Library.

Acknowledgements
We would like to thank the following for permission to reproduce photographs: ©agefotostock pp. **16** (Image Source/Royalty Free), **20** (John Birdsall); ©drr.net pp. **10** (Borut Peterlin), **11** (Huntstock.com), **14** (enzodalverme.com), **15** (Image Source Ltd.), **23 bottom** (enzodalverme. com); ©Getty Images pp. **4** (Ryan McVay), **7** (Chris Cheadle), **9** (David Deas), **13** (Paul Viant), **19** (Jacobs Stock Photography); ©Heinemann Raintree p. **6** (Richard Hutchings); ©istockphoto p. **17** (ranplett); ©Jupiter Images p. **21** (Comma Image); ©PhotoEdit pp. **22** (Michael Newman), **23 middle** (Michael Newman); ©Shutterstock pp. **8** (Amra Pasic), **12** (Ronen), **23 top** (Ronen).

Cover photograph of hearing and speech impaired students interacting with each other using sign language reproduced with permission of ©AP Photo (Mahesh Kumar A). Back cover photograph of a family talking reproduced with permission of ©Shutterstock (Rob Marmion).

Every effort has been made to contact copyright holders of material reproduced in this book. Any omissions will be rectified in subsequent printings if notice is given to the publishers.

Disclaimer
All the Internet addresses (URLs) given in this book were valid at the time of going to press. However, due to the dynamic nature of the Internet, some addresses may have changed, or sites may have changed or ceased to exist since publication. While the author and Publishers regret any inconvenience this may cause readers, no responsibility for any such changes can be accepted by either the author or the Publishers.

Contents

Differences

4

We are all different ages and sizes. We all have different coloured hair and skin. We are all good at different things.

Communicating

People communicate in
different ways.

People understand in different ways.

Listening

Sometimes people listen to loud sounds.

Sometimes people listen to
quiet sounds.

Sometimes people listen to
their teacher.

Sometimes people listen to
their friends.

headphones

Sometimes people listen to a television.

Sometimes people listen to a radio.

Talking

People talk in different ways. Some people talk using sign language.

People talk in different places.

Sometimes people shout in
loud voices.

Sometimes people whisper in soft voices.

Sometimes people talk to
their family.

Sometimes people talk to
their neighbours.

We are all different

We are all different.

How do you talk? How do you listen?

Words to know

 **headphones** small speakers people wear over or inside the ears. Headphones help people hear.

 **hearing aid** small machine that helps people hear. Hearing aids fit inside and behind the ear.

 **sign language** way to talk with hand signs

This section includes related vocabulary words that can help children learn about this topic. Use these words to explore communication.

Index

Note to parents and teachers
Before reading
Talk with children about the ways we are the same and different. Discuss how some of the differences are physical or mental and some are because different people like different things, but that all people are special and all people are equally important.

After reading
Ask children to list as many ways to communicate as they can think of (e.g. writing emails, talking on the telephone, sign language). Then ask the children to vote on their favourite way to communicate. Record the answers on the board.